D1475419

Blue Book

Veuve
Clicquot
Champagne

Yellow Label "Sec"
Gold Label "Brut"

THE HIGHEST GRADE OF
CHAMPAGNE PRODUCED

Blue Book

APPLEWOOD
AFTER DARK

Carlisle, Massachusetts

ISBN 978-1-4290-9328-6

10 9 8 7 6 5 4 3 2 1

MANUFACTURED IN
THE UNITED STATES OF AMERICA
WITH AMERICAN-MADE MATERIALS

PUBLISHER'S INTRODUCTION (2013)

This Blue Book *is a reproduction of a copy owned by Judith Lafitte of New Orleans. Judith and her husband, Tom Lowenburg, opened Octavia Books, located in uptown New Orleans, in 2000. Not only is Octavia a great independent bookstore, recognized nationally, but it has become an important community center and a vocal advocate for free speech. Judith was given this copy of the book by her mother's third husband, Joseph Arnoult. It had been given to Joseph by his father as a rite of passage at the innocent age of 14. A single check mark, the only handwriting in the book, was found alongside one of the "residents." Judith's copy is extremely valuable today as a collectible, a souvenir, and a historic record.*

The Blue Book *was a famous guidebook—actually a series of guidebooks—to New Orleans's vice district, Storyville. It was published in various editions from about 1909 to 1915 by Billy Struve or "Billy News," a former police reporter for the New Orleans Daily Item. Struve, as you can see on the advertisement for Alexander's Saloon, also managed the saloon owned by Thomas C. Alexander, whom many called the "Mayor of Storyville." Struve printed the* Blue Book *in a shop located on the second floor of a building on the corner of Basin Street and Bienville, right above Lulu White's famous saloon and next door to White's Mahogany Hall. Very few copies of the* Blue Book *have survived, as it was used and discarded.*

The Blue Book *is considered one of New Orleans's most important books, telling the story of the place in a way that only a practical and useful book can. Of course, it is only useful today in opening a window on a neighborhood now gone, as Storyville was closed down by the U.S. government in 1917, in an effort to make New Orleans a safe port of debarkation for soldiers in World War I. According to Storyville historian Dr. Alecia Long, Martin Behrman, the mayor of New Orleans at the time said, "You can make prostitution illegal in Louisiana, but you can't make it unpopular."*

Our mission is to build a picture of America through its primary sources. We do that without changing a word. Our reproduction of the Blue Book *is intended to be a window onto a New Orleans—its people and places—that is now gone. We have taken tremendous care to present this book as it was. We hope you enjoy our efforts.*

—Applewood Books, September 2013

PREFACE

THIS Directory and Guide of the Sporting District has been before the people on many occasions, and has proven its authority as to what is doing in the "Queer Zone."

Anyone who knows to-day from yesterday will say that the Blue Book is the right book for the right people.

WHY NEW ORLEANS SHOULD HAVE THIS DIRECTORY

Because it is the only district of its kind in the States set aside for the fast women by law.

Because it puts the stranger on a proper and safe path as to where he may go and be free from "Hold-ups," and other games usually practiced upon the stranger.

It regulates the women so that they may live in one district to themselves instead of being scattered over the city and filling our thoroughfares with street walkers.

It also gives the names of women entertainers employed in the Dance Halls and Cabarets in the District.

THIS BOOK MUST NOT BE MAILED

To KNOW the right from the wrong, to be sure of yourself, go through this little book and read it carefully, and then when you visit Storyville you will know the best places to spend your money and time, as all the BEST houses are advertised. Read all the "ads."

This book contains nothing but Facts, and is of the greatest value to strangers when in this part of the city. The names of the residents will be found in this Directory, alphabetically arranged, under the headings "White" and "Colored," from alpha to omega. The names in capitals are landladies only.

You will find the boundary of the Tenderloin District, or Storyville: North side Iberville Street to south side St. Louis, and east side North Basin to west side North Robertson Street.

This is the boundary in which the women are compelled to live, according to law.

Geo. A. Dickel & Co.

Cascade

[DISTILLERY]

HAND-MADE
SOUR MASH

Tennessee
Whiskey

F. HOLLANDER & CO.
DISTRIBUTORS   NEW ORLEANS

LETTER "A" (WHITE)

Allen, Mary	225 N. Basin
Adams, Nan	225 N. Basin
Anderson, Evelyn	315 N. Franklin
Abadie, Ritta	211 Marais
Arnold, Evelyn	315 N. Basin
Anderson, Willie	226 Marais
Alier, Martha	1200 Iberville
Adams, Mary	1549 Iberville

LETTER "B" (WHITE)

Byrd, Stella	1423 Iberville
Burns, Billy	1547 Iberville
Bose, Anna	1208 Bienville
Baker, Mabel	1306 Bienville
Bonafon, Bella	1305 Bienville
Brady, Rosie	1309 Bienville
Bossie, Laura	1507 Bienville
Butler, Camelia	1528 Conti
Baily, May	1556 Conti
Bagarter, Elizabeth	1557 Conti
Brown, Annie	1409 Iberville
Bloom, Mauna	1319 Iberville
Brown, Josephine	1208 Iberville
Bella, Anna	1211 Iberville
Buges, Helen	1217 Iberville
Barrymore, Bennie	1302 Iberville
Black, Ida	1302 ½ Iberville
Brooks, Belle	1313 Iberville

El Jar

10 Cent Cigar

Cost the **Dealer**
More
Same Price to
You

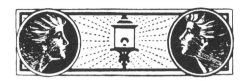

LETTER "B" (WHITE)—Continued

Brown, Sadie	1321 Iberville
Bloom, Rosie	1305½ Iberville
Bush, May	1410 Iberville
Brown, Tillie	1412 Iberville
Burke, Marie	1421½ Iberville
Brown, Jessie	223 N. Basin
Boyer, Edna	223 N. Basin
Borris, Rose	319 N. Basin
Baker, Louise	325 N. Basin
Bradley, Mabel	331 N. Basin
BROWN, JESSIE	215½ N. Franklin
Bailey, Theresa	228 N. Franklin
Brownie, Louise	230 N. Franklin
Belmont, Lillie	319 Marais
Burnett, Hazle	1320 Bienville

LETTER "C" (WHITE)

Cale, Elsie	209 N. Basin
CASEY, ANNA	225 N. Basin
Caruth, Edith	311 N. Basin
Caruth, Pauline	311 N. Basin
Carter, Snooks	320 N. Franklin
Cohen, Georgie	315 N. Franklin
Cullum, Ruby	1304 Conti
Clark, Martha	327 N. Basin
Calamese, Donna	321 N. Basin
Cohen, Dora	205½ N. Franklin
Cohen, Fannie	215 N. Franklin

Substantial Quality

𝕶𝖎𝖓𝖌𝖘 𝕮𝖔𝖚𝖗𝖙

ROYAL CIGARS

Cardinal Size
5 Cents Straight

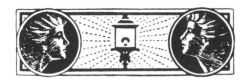

LETTER "C" (WHITE)—Continued

Clark, Tuts	217 N. Franklin
Chandler, Josie	323 Marais
Callaghan, Nell	1318 Bienville
Casler, Ritta	1313 Bienville
Chanore, Rachael	1529 Conti
Crawford, Alice	1556 Conti
Clarke, Toots	1316 Iberville

LETTER "D" (WHITE)

DIX, GERTRUDE	209 N. Basin
Duncan, Dorothy	225 N. Basin
De Jardin, Violatte	231 N. Basin
Devons, Aileen	320 N. Franklin
Druary, Nellie	311 N. Franklin
Davis, Rose	1304 Conti
Davis, Jennie	213 N. Franklin
Davis, Ruby	219 N. Franklin
Devine, Edna	229 N. Franklin
DAVIS, DAISY	210 Marais
Dupre, Camile	222 Marais
Dupre, Emelie	318 Marais
Danton, Emma	226 Marais
Denorms, Gabriel	1202½ Iberville
Dubois, Lilac	1202 Iberville
Darley, Paullette	1216 Iberville
De Belle, Anna	1308 Iberville
Davis, Lena	1402 Iberville
Dayton, Lee	1421 Iberville

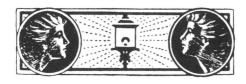

LETTER "D" (WHITE)—Continued

Donne, Rose	1215 Bienville
Dickson, Frankie	1306½ Bienville
Douglas, Jean	1318 Bienville
Desmond, Laura	1320 Conti
Desmond, Mattie	1508 Conti
Deffes, Marie	1528 Conti
Davis, Ella	1528 Conti

LETTER "E" (WHITE)

Easterling, Aline	209 N. Basin
EVANS, MAY	315 N. Basin
Evans, Jessie	217 N. Franklin
Evans, Mabel	1312 Bienville
Evans, May	1550 Conti
Elliott, Percy	1510 St. Louis

LETTER "F" (WHITE)

Farleigh, Ethel	225 N. Basin
Fielure, Sophie	335 N. Franklin
Fuller, Ethel	207½ N. Franklin
Fruma, Hilda	227 N. Franklin
Felix, Mrs. Sam	219 N. Liberty
Floyd, Unice	226 N. Villere
Foster, Mary	1307 Iberville
Flood, Virgie	1303 Iberville
Ferrer, Mildred	1530 Bienville
Frumenthal, Alvera	1540 Bienville
Frank, Lula	1530 Conti

Ruy Lopez Cigars

Key West, Florida

Valloft & Dreux

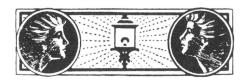

LETTER "F" (WHITE)—Continued

Fuchette, Julia   1550 Conti
Friedburg, Sadie   1314 Iberville

LETTER "G" (WHITE)

Griffin, Marguerite   221 N. Basin
Gay, Mayorie   225 N. Basin
Gilbert, Frances   307 N. Basin
Grunewald, Maud   341 N. Basin
Gibson, Dorothy   1304 Conti
Grand, Henrietta   318 Marais
Grice, Ida   319 N. Villere
Gray, Dorothy   1309 Iberville
Guria, Dora   1315 Iberville
Green, Ida   1301½ Iberville
Girard, Clara   1414 Iberville
Gordon, Tessie   1408 Iberville
Gold, Rosie   1417 Iberville
Geary, Ella   1538 Iberville
Gilmore, May   1563 Iberville
Gatwright, Nettie   1526 Conti
Gordon, Alice   1521 Conti
Griffin, Maud   1549 Conti
Green, Sadie   1312½ Iberville

LETTER "H" (WHITE)

Hall, Edna   221 N. Basin
Hartell, Jane   221 N. Basin
Hayes, Ada   341 N. Basin

Practices in All Courts

P. L. Fourchy

Attorney and Counsellor-at-Law

Residence: 1330 Hospital St.
Phone Hemlock 1267-L

Office Hours: 8 to 10 a. m.
Phone Main 3585   3 to 4 p. m.

Office: 127 Carondelet Street

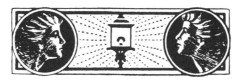

LETTER "H" (WHITE)—Continued

HARTMANN, MAUD	327 N. Franklin
Hilton, Maud	327 N. Franklin
HAMILTON, EDNA	1304 Conti
Hoffmann, Louise	231 N. Franklin
Hill, Cora	224 N. Franklin
Hoppe, Pauline	223 Marais
Howard, Grace	226 N. Villere
Hall, Sylvia	1400 Iberville
Harris, Hazel	1403½ Iberville
Hunt, Helen	1407 Iberville
Hess, Catherine	1425 Iberville
Howard, Marguerite	1427 Iberville
Hyatt, Julia	1437 Iberville
Hastings, May	1427½ Iberville
Haydell, May	1536 Iberville
Hayer, Pauline	1304 Bienville
Hart, Rosie	1320 Conti
HOLLAND, HARRIET	1318 Bienville
Hennessey, Alice	1547 Conti
Holmes, Minnie	1311 Iberville

LETTER "J" (WHITE)

JOHNSON, EMMA	331 N. Basin
Johnson, Anna	341 N. Basin
Jones, Louise	307 N. Villere
Johnson, Mabel	1545 Iberville
Jacobson, Ida	1212 Bienville
Johnson, Florence	1320 Conti
Johnson, Florence	1528 Conti
Junice, Mary	1557 Conti

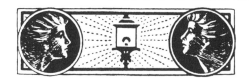

LETTER "K" (WHITE)

Kline, Louise	229 N. Basin
Kennedy, Josephine	311 N. Basin
Kline, Jennie	1304½ Iberville
Kugler, Ida	1410½ Iberville
King, Marie	1320 Conti
Kline, Rosie	1557 Conti
Klein, Frances	217 N. Franklin
Klein, Jennie	1416 Iberville

LETTER "L" (WHITE)

Lucas, Marianne	1318 Bienville
Lawrence, Rosie	1313 Bienville
Laramme, Madelene	221 N. Basin
Love, Grace	223 N. Basin
Le Blond, Marcelle	305 N. Basin
LODIE, OLGA	321 N. Basin
LLOYD, GRACE	338 N. Franklin
Lister, Nellie	338 N. Franklin
Lovejoy, Lois	207 N. Franklin
Lamarque, Nathalie	219½ N. Franklin
Levy, Helen	229½ N. Franklin
Livingston, Flossie	226 N. Villere
Leroy, Annie	1214 Iberville
Lee, Mary	1304 Iberville
Lambert, Camile	1433 Iberville
Leroy, Edna	1437 Iberville
Lawrence, Adeline	1536 Iberville
Lloyd, Estelle	1537 Iberville

Webster Havana Cigars

MOTTO

QUALITY

Y. PENDAS & ALVAREZ
Makers

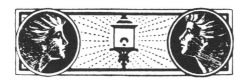

LETTER "L" (WHITE)—Continued

Long, King	1549 Iberville
Lee, Rose	1559 Iberville
Lester, Ruby	1425 Iberville
Leon, Josephine	1306 Bienville

LETTER "M" (WHITE)

Miller, Leah	223 N. Liberty
Milton, Mildred	315 N. Basin
Mazelle, Wanita	1215 Iberville
Miller, Annie	1310 Iberville
McEwen, Lee	1320 Iberville
Martin, Stella	1309½ Iberville
Miller, Teddy	1415 Iberville
McCoy, Helen	1540 Iberville
Morris, Mildred	1559 Iberville
Milto, Violet	1310½ Bienville
Miller, Annabelle	1318 Bienville
Miller, Annie	1313 Bienville
Marrelton, Antonie	1509 Bienville
MORRIS, FRANCES	1320 Conti
Mosely, Carne	1320 Conti
Miller, Martha	1524 Conti
Mirandy, Lena	1550 Conti
Milington, Bobbie	1554 Conti
Moore, Bessie	209 N. Basin
Miller, Ada	209 N. Basin
Milton, Ivy	223 N. Basin
Marlowe, Adelle	331 N. Basin

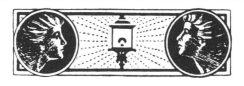

LETTER "M" (WHITE)—Continued

Morris, Viola	209 N. Franklin
Meyers, Marguerite	213 N. Franklin
Morgan, Nora	1567 Conti
Meyers, Ruby	1540 St. Louis
Mason, Adelle	1211 Iberville

LETTER "N" (WHITE)

Noon, Annie	227 N. Franklin
Nonia, Julia	318 N. Marais
Norton, Ollie	322 Marais
Nolan, Alica	315 N. Villere
Nesbit, Evelyn	1414 Iberville
Naoh, Nana	1315 Bienville

LETTER "O" (WHITE)

O'Dowd, Madge	1547 Iberville
O'BRIEN, MAY	1547 Iberville
O'Reilley, Ketty	1312 Conti

LETTER "P" (WHITE)

Pittman, Marguerite	209 N. Basin
Powers, Florence	225 N. Basin
Patterson, Ida	209½ N. Franklin
Petit, Marcelle	1202 Iberville
Patton, May	1219 Iberville
Palmer, Mabel	1300 Iberville
Pascal, Rosy	1406 Iberville
Pascal, Josephine	1420 Iberville

LETTER "P" (WHITE)—Continued

Palmer, Jeannette	1403 Iberville
Price, Sadie	1536 Iberville
Powell, Louise	1536 Iberville
Parker, Bessie	1300 Bienville
Petit, Myrtle	1306 Bienville

LETTER "R" (WHITE)

Rhea, Glady	1554 Conti
Refell, Bonita	225 N. Basin
Rose, Violet	209 N. Basin
RAY, DIANA	213 N. Basin
Reed, Florence	223 N. Basin
Raymond, Nell	223 N. Basin
Rocco, Rita	321 N. Basin
Russell, Glady	331 N. Basin
Roe, Marguerite	315 N. Franklin
Rice, Ruby	315 N. Franklin
Rivers, Edith	327 N. Franklin
Ruttan, Stella	1311½ Iberville
Rice, Helen	1311 Iberville
Rose, Annie	1536 Iberville
Russell, Katie	1538 Iberville
Reed, Marguerite	1537 Iberville
Ross, Josephine	1545 Iberville
Randolph, Estelli	1547 Iberville
RAYMOND, LOU	1563 Iberville
Robertson, Eva	1510 Conti
Ray, Jessie	1542 Conti
Robertson, Marguerite	1542 Conti

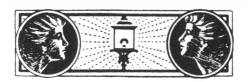

LETTER "S" (WHITE)

Smith, Victoria	1302½ Iberville
Stone, Claudie	1310 Iberville
Stern, Mary	1312 Iberville
Smith, Annie	1303½ Iberville
Silbeman, Lena	1311 Iberville
Smith, Marie	1317 Iberville
Straus, Beatrice	1319 Iberville
Singer, Katie	1323 Iberville
Smith, Mary	1406½ Iberville
Spence, Bertha	1424 Iberville
Shiloski, Ida	1415 Iberville
Savignic, Jane	1419 Iberville
Stevens, Virgie	1210½ Iberville
Shepherd, Myrtle	1536 Iberville
SMITH, MARY	1538 Iberville
Standford, Eva	1559 Iberville
Strohmeyer, Nelle	1302 Bienville
Scott, Minnie	1310½ Bienville
Schnect, Rosie	1314 Bienville
Stanley, Vira	1318 Bienville
SMITH, LIZETTE	217 N. Basin
Sherley, Liza	225 N. Basin
Stein, Rose	307 N. Basin
Smith, Alma	325 N. Basin
Smith, Evelyn	325 N. Basin
Smith, Gertrude	341 N. Basin
Stanley, Inez	338 N. Franklin
Sarlie, Trixie	315 N. Franklin

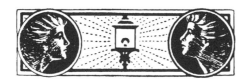

LETTER "S" (WHITE)—Continued

Spencer, Marie	225 N. Franklin
Smith, Gertrude	206 N. Liberty
Schneider, Ida	215 N. Liberty
Sanders, Louise	210 N. Marais
Shay, Vic	216 N. Marais
Shay, Rose	222 N. Marais
Simmons, Rose	222 N. Marais
Sawyer, Frances	315 N. Basin
SPENCER, MAY	315 N. Basin
Smith, Viola	318 N. Marais
Smith, Jeannette	1204 Iberville
Smith, Lucy	1212 Iberville
Stemloger, Wilemen	1411 Bienville
Smith, Ida	1527 Bienville
Smith, May	1520 Conti
Schultz, Louise	1526 Conti
Smith, Edna	1528 Conti
Smith, Rosie	1313 Iberville

LETTER "T" (WHITE)

Turner, Alice	215 N. Basin
Thurston, Florence	1206 Iberville
Tracy, Susie	1210 Iberville
Tanner, Ruby	1405½ Iberville
Tagent, Julia	1540 Iberville
Tuckerman, May	1549 Iberville
Tyra, Ruby	1410 Bienville
Tracy, Della	1320 Conti

"*Have a Chatt*"

Imperial Pilsener
Zacherl Brau
and
Reifo Standard

BREWED BY
Chattanooga Brewing Co.
BOTTLED ONLY AT THE BREWERY

Yochim Bros. Co., Ltd., Distributors
534-536 Bienville St.   Phone Main 2429

LETTER "T" (WHITE)—Continued

Thompson, Lottie	1549 Conti
Thow, Frances	1316 Iberville

LETTER "U" (WHITE)

Ulmar, Maud	1306½ Bienville

LETTER "V" (WHITE)

Vernon, Lena	226 Marais

LETTER "W" (WHITE)

WHITE, Minnie	221 N. Basin
Wilson, Louise	221 N. Basin
Wright, Check	223 N. Basin
Watson, Goldie	223 N. Basin
WEINTHAL, BERTHA	311 N. Basin
Walker, Rita	311 N. Basin
Wilson, May	331 N. Basin
Walker, Edna	327 N. Franklin
Wilson, Bessie	205 N. Franklin
Wilson, May	215 N. Franklin
Wallace, Katie	216 N. Marais
Williams, Lillie	325 N. Marais
Winifred, Woo	1213 Iberville
Wright, Billy	1310½ Iberville
Williams, Lottie	1303 Iberville
Wilson, Kitty	1307½ Iberville
White, Sadie	1408 Iberville
Williams, Grace	1536 Iberville

Here Is the Winner!
HANOVER
═ RYE ═

HANOVER

Sold in the best Cafes
and Cabarets to the
Best People who know
the "VERIBEST."

FRANK LONG
REPRESENTATIVE

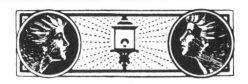

LETTER "W" (WHITE)—Continued

Williams, Frances	1538 Iberville
Williams, Alice	1545 Iberville
Woods, Hazel	1547 Iberville
Ward, Adelle	1549 Iberville
Wagner, Helen	1549 Iberville
Wells, Dolly	1309 Iberville
Williams, Ida	1300 Bienville
Watkins, Clara	1300 Bienville
White, Maud	1308 Bienville
White, Lillie	1312 Bienville
Whiteman, Jane	1318 Bienville
Ward, Grace	1303 Bienville
Washburn, Bessie	1307 Bienville
Woods, Alina	1426½ Bienville
Wilson, Sadie	1405 Bienville
West, Annie	1524 Conti
Wright, Daisy	1526 Conti
Wallace, Laura	426 Robertson
Williams, Anna	1304 Iberville
Ware, Marie	213 N. Basin
Weise, Annie	1426 Iberville

ABSOLUTELY
UNEQUALLED

ALISA

HAVANA
CIGARS

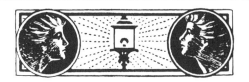

LATE ARRIVALS

Jennie Schneider	205 N. Franklin
Camille Franklin	223 N. Basin
Dorothy Hale	223 N. Basin
Thelma Morris	216 Marais
Mabel Veirs	209 N. Basin
Ruth Cook	225 N. Basin
Elton Taylor	315 N. Basin
Marie Smith	321 N. Basin
Katie Strickland	1504 Conti
Lucille Smith	445 N. Robertson
Ethel Gray	216 N. Liberty
Pearl Leonard	1302 Bienville
Jeanette Weaver	225 N. Basin
Heather White	225 N. Basin
May Davitt	226 N. Frankiln
Eva Miller	224 N. Rampart
Doris Arnolds	1427 Iberville
Virgie Hunter	1005½ Iberville
Edna Brown	1406½ Iberville
Tony Lameithe	1304 Conti
Mary Brown	1302 Bienville
Jeanne Clifford	217 N. Franklin

LATE ARRIVALS—Continued

Eleonora Dunn	218 N. Robertson
Jane Waitleman	1318 Bienville
Annabelle Miller	1318 Bienville
Anna Laura Richardson	218 N. Franklin
Blanche Bohling	223 N. Franklin
Minnie Hahne	1311 Iberville
Adelle Mason	1310 Iberville
Nathalie A. Albright	209 N. Basin
Pearl Smith	315 N. Basin
Helen Rice	219 N. Liberty
Lucile Warner	223 N. Basin
Ellen Brooks	223 N. Basin
Nellie Taylor	223 N. Basin
Pearl White	1426½ Iberville
Francis Miller	215 N. Franklin
Helen Leroy	320 N. Franklin
Ruby Clarke	217 N. Franklin
Ruby Willard	209 N. Basin
Vera Miller	341 N. Basin
Anita Smith (colored)	1420 Conti
Dora Thompson (colored)	1522 Iberville
Mamie Floyd (colored)	1424 Bienville
Bertha Revel (colored)	1424 Bienville

King of Table Waters

King of Table Waters

TRY THE NEW

El Príncipe

de Gales

Clear Havana
Cigars

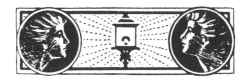

OCTOROONS

PIAZZA, WILLIE   317 N. Basin

Carter, Iris   317 N. Basin

Hamilton, Held Lee   317 N. Basin

Miller, Sweety   317 N. Basin

Sherer, Madie   317 N. Basin

WHITE, LULU   235 N. Basin

Porter, Florence   235 N. Basin

Vindabel, Queen   235 N. Basin

Williams, Minnie   235 N. Basin

Alhambra Baths

IME and again the Turkish, Russian and Electric Light Baths, together with exercise, massage and diet have proven their efficiency in the relief of these diseases: Gouty Conditions, Rheumatism, Skin Troubles, Stomach Disorders, Constipation, Obesity, Biliousness, Neurasthenia, Insomnia, Colds, Nausea, Dyspepsia, Liver Troubles and Bright's Disease.

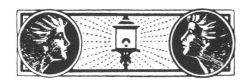

LETTER "A" (COLORED)

Adams, Tillie	229 N. Liberty
Allen, Patsy	324 N. Robertson
Allen, Florine	326 N. Robertson
Anthony, Marie	1504 Iberville
Allen, Rosie	1507 Iberville
Anderson, Elizabeth	1402 Bienville
Anderson, Bessie	1523 Bienville
Allen, Frances	1501 Conti
Alapender, Lula	1503 Conti
Anderson, Pauline	1571 Conti
Allen, Maude	1504 Conti

LETTER "B" (COLORED)

Bryant, Mary	227 N. Liberty
Bailey, Bertha	325 N. Liberty
Brown, Alice	322 N. Marais
Berry, Lillie	229 N. Villere
Breaux, Florena	226 N. Robertson
Brown, Mammie	320 N. Robertson
Brown, Bessie	324 N. Robertson
Brown, Mabel	1202 Iberville
Brown, Rosy	1428 Iberville
Burns, Albertha	1516 Iberville
Buce, Ruby	1503 Iberville
Bartholomew, Edna	1511 Iberville
Brants, Lillie	1531 Iberville
Bell, Mabel	1533 Iberville
Brown, Effie	1314 Bienville

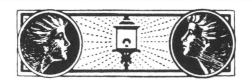

LETTER "B" (COLORED)—Continued

Blanchard, Camille	1404 Bienville
Brown, Eleonore	1528 Bienville
Beck, Jessie	1530 Bienville
Brooks, Ethel	1506 Conti
Baptiste, Elizabeth	1426 St. Louis
Bertholemew, Mary	1544 St. Louis

LETTER "C" (COLORED)

Cammack, Mamie	339 N. Liberty
Callaway, Nita	315 N. Liberty
Coleman, Lillie	225 N. Villere
Clark, Alma	214 N. Robertson
Chambers, Albertha	314 N. Robertson
Carter, Lizzie	1402 Iberville
Clay, Camille	1507 Iberville
Christmas, Bessie	1533 Iberville
Coleman, Liza	1533 Iberville
Charles, Mathilda	1410 Bienville
Cherie, Elizabeth	1422½ Bienville
Conrad, Anna	1518 Bienville
Crawford, Stella	1524 Bienville
Cook, Mary	1325 Conti
Cailloux, Victoria	328 N. Robertson

LETTER "D" (COLORED)

Davis, Eleonore	16 N. Robertson
Dickerson, Viola	216 N. Robertson
Dorsey, Carrie	426 N. Villere

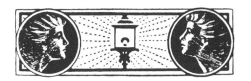

LETTER "D" (COLORED)—Continued

Davis, Nita	1402 Iberville
Dyer, Florence	1504 Iberville
Dumas, Jane	1410 Bienville
Dominick, Julia	1424 Bienville
Dunlap, Martha	1427 Bienville
Davis, Mary	1515 Bienville
Donnett, Alfa	1544 Bienville
Dreyfus, Louise	1310 Conti
Dickson, Mary	1418 Conti
De Verges, Rosetta	1426 Conti
Duvalle, Carrie	1416 St. Louis

LETTER "E" (COLORED)

Evans, Josephine	1412 Bienville
Easley, Mary	1519 Bienville
Edward, Edna	1527 Bienville
Esperon, Claudie	1565 Conti

LETTER "F" (COLORED)

Foley, Mary	230 N. Robertson
Fisher, Cora	1529 Iberville
Foley, Olivia	1565 Iberville
Frazier, Ollie	1522 Bienville
Franklin, Bertha	1519 Bienville
Foster, Alice	1551 Bienville
Fitch, Rosie	1530 St. Louis

BUY HER

Jacob's

DELICIOUS CANDIES

"MADE LAST NIGHT"

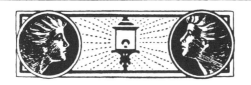

LETTER "G" (COLORED)

Griffin, Inez	320 N. Robertson
Green, Acy Lena	1424½ Iberville
Gray, Alice	1416½ Bienville
Grant, Anna	1426 Bienville
Gabriel, Emely	1415 Bienville
Green, Gabriel	1504 Bienville
George, Mabel	1511 Bienville
Gonzales, Wanita	1308 Conti
Gardner, Lucy	1540 Conti
Green, Virginia	1546 Conti

LETTER "H" (COLORED)

Harris, Mary	333 N. Liberty
Hayes, Emma	331 N. Liberty
Hubbard, Annie	408 N. Robertson
Henderson, Bertha	1429 Iberville
Harrison, Mammie	1323 Bienville
Hamilton, Catherine	1425 Bienville
Hesten, Augustine	1410 Conti
Holmes, Alice	1503 Conti
Hilma, Ada	1523 Conti
Hartford, Marianne	1420 St. Louis

LETTER "I" (COLORED)

Ingram, Delia	1564 Conti

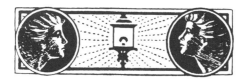

LETTER "J" (COLORED)

Johnson, Rosabelle	337	N. Liberty
Jones, Bettie	333	N. Liberty
Jackson, Laura	309	N. Liberty
Jackson, Eleonora	213	N. Marais
Jackson, Hattie	322	N. Villere
Jackson, Johnnie	214	N. Robertson
Jefferson, Mary	1531	Iberville
Johnson, Irene	1533	Iberville
Joseph, Della	1533	Iberville
Johnson, Florida	1533	Iberville
Jacobs, Alice	1567	Iberville
Jones, Lettie	1321	Bienville
Jones, Annabelle	1406	Bienville
Jacobs, Myrtle	1406	Bienville
Jupiter, Mabel	1410	Bienville
Jones, Ella	1426	Bienville
Joseph, Theresa	1417	Bienville
Jackson, Gladys	1520	Bienville
Johnson, Ids	1517	Bienville
Jackson, Mary	1564	Bienville
Jackson, Carrie	1551	Bienville
Johnson, Florence	1518	Conti
Johnson, Sylvia	1558	Conti
Jackson, Melvine	1408	St. Louis
Johnson, Catherine	1512	St. Louis
Johnson, Louise	1512	St. Louis

Preferencia Cigars

A
MILD
S
M
O
K
E

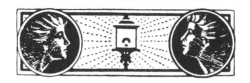

LETTER "K" (COLORED)

Kelly, Eleonore	208½ N. Liberty
Kelly, Beatrice	1411 Iberville
King, Malinda	1506 St. Louis
Kaigler, Wanita	1518 St. Louis

LETTER "L" (COLORED)

Lee, Paty	214 N. Robertson
Lee, Thelma	314 N. Robertson
Lewis, Vivienne	320 N. Robertson
Lawson, Julia	414 N. Robertson
Lewis, Nita	1414½ Iberville
Laws, Leona	1516½ Iberville
Lewis, Lucile	1520 Iberville
Lee, Elizabeth	1552 Iberville
Louis, Monah	1406 Bienville
Lee, Rosa	1550 Bienville
Lewis, Evelyna	1426 Conti
Lucien, Anita	1433 Conti
Lucien, Louise	1431 Conti
Lowey, Robertha	1410 St. Louis

LETTER "M" (COLORED)

Morgan, Mandy	333 N. Liberty
Morgan, Ester	319 N. Liberty
Morris, Agnes	213 Marais
Moore, Hazel	320 N. Robertson
Moore, Ida	1518 Iberville
McCoy, Blanche	1507 Iberville

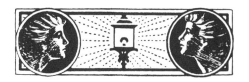

LETTER "M" (COLORED)—Continued

Monroe, Corinne	1519 Iberville
Marks, Edna	1519 Iberville
Malone, Bertha	1521 Iberville
Mosely, Mary	1529½ Iberville
Moore, Mattie	1531 Iberville
McGee, Eliza	1567 Iberville
Monnier, Elizabeth	1418 Bienville
Messina, Blanche	1418½ Bienville
Morgan, Stella	1528 Bienville
McDonald, Mary	1517 Bienville
McClaud, Pauline	1517 Bienville
Moore, Emma	1552 Bienville
Mitchell, Alma	1566 Bienville
McCoy, Rosie	1551 Bienville
Mendoza, Leah	324 N. Franklin
Mendez, Chiquita	1310 Conti
Martinez, Jennie	1426 Conti
Moseby, Talie	1514 St. Louis

LETTER "O" (COLORED)

Owmes, Louise	314 N. Robertson

LETTER "P" (COLORED)

Prevost, Mary	318 N. Liberty
Penera, Ella	228 N. Robertson
Paul, Gertrude	1402 Iberville
Pecou, Rebecca	1504 Iberville
Palmer, Bertha	1520 Iberville

Portina
Cigars

KEEP UP
THEIR
QUALITY

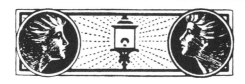

LETTER "P" (COLORED)—Continued

Perey, Frances	1509 Iberville
Polite, Victoria	1531 Iberville
Plunket, Carrie	1413 Bienville
Porter, Sarah	1522 Bienville
Prim, Mary	1418 Conti
Perry, Alice	1420 Conti
Pender, Gertrude	1501 Conti

LETTER "R" (COLORED)

Ross, Laura	331 N. Liberty
Roberts, Emma	204 Marais
Robertson, Lottie	228 N. Villere
Ralton, Felicie	225 N. Villere
Richdson, Annie Lon	218 N. Robertson
Rose, Mary	314 N. Robertson
Reiley, Cornelia	324 N. Robertson
Raymond, Rachel	414 N. Robertson
Richardson, Lola	1409½ Iberville
Rochelle, Fannie	1525 Bienville
Richardson, Lizzie	1527 Bienville
Robertson, Lizzie	1508 St. Louia

LETTER "S" (COLORED)

Sanders, Maggie	231 N. Liberty
Songas, Maggie	333 N. Liberty
Stanton, Lottie	218 N. Robertson
Sanders, Vivienne	324 N. Robertson
Schleet, Cora	326 N. Robertson

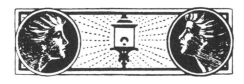

LETTER "S" (COLORED)—Continued

Stein, Mabel	1426½ Iberville
Strodder, Annie	1505 Iberville
Shaffer, Henrietta	1423 Bienville
Stewart, Irene	1423 Bienville
Smooth, Edna	1522 Bienville
Simms, Liza	1524 Bienville
Smith, Pearl	1550 Bienville
Sanders, Marie	1412 St. Louis
Stanton, Lottie	224 N. Robertson

LETTER "T" (COLORED)

Tolmaire, Winnie	232 N. Robertson
Turner, Camille	319 N. Basin
Taylor, Dora	1521 Iberville
Thompson, Dora	1533 Iberville
Thomas, Stella	1422 Bienville
Taylor, Evelyn	1515 Bienville
Taylor, Frances	1525 Conti
Taylor, Edna	1525 Conti

LETTER "V" (COLORED)

Vance, Orphilia	1519 Iberville
Villa, Ernestine	1400 Bienville

None Better

Old Saratoga
Rye

*Sold at Tom
Anderson's
Bars and
Other First
Class Places*

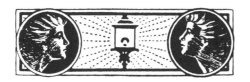

LETTER "W" (COLORED)

Walter, Louise	208 N. Liberty
Williams, Mollie	319 N. Liberty
Washington, Ruby	216 N. Liberty
Webb, Albertha	234 N. Robertson
White, Sadie	326 N. Robertson
Watkins, Evelyn	1576 Iberville
Wallace, Georgie	1520 Iberville
Wilson, Lucy	1521 Iberville
Williams, Dora	1521 Iberville
Wynn, Cleo	1424 Bienville
Williams, Bertha	1411 Bienville
Williams, Olivia	1526 Bienville
Williams, Essie	1530 Bienville
Williams, Mabel	1504 Conti
White, Lizzie	1501 Conti
Wilson, Mildred	1501 Conti
White, Sarah	1540 Conti
Williams, Sarah	1542 Conti
Wilson, Mary	1546 Conti
Ward, Ellen	1566 Conti
Woods, Lucinda	1430 St. Louis
Williams, Alice	212 N. Robertson

LETTER "Y" (COLORED)

Young, Rena	1420 St. Louis
Yarber Lovina	1556 St. Louis

CASINO CABARET, 1400 Iberville Street
(White)

Lottie Gaines	Maxime Hiell	Estelle Jones
Isabella Gray	Lula Stanley	Mabel Conroy
Elma Frey	Ethel White	Alma Murray
Mary Mouton	Maud Henry	Cleo Flynn

ABADIE CABARET, 1501 Bienville Street
(White)

Laura Chester	Mamie Carlton	Lillie Johnson
Cy. Chester		Violet Seymour

MY PLACE CABARET, 1216 Bienville Street
(White)

Julia Nelson	Viola Donovan	Abby Duffy
Philomina Dupre	Florence Marino	Gertie Golden
Tillie Gates		Clara Murphy

UNION CABARET, 135 North Basin Street
(White)

Hazel Bradburry	Ruby Smith	Stella Kennedy
Ada White	Theresa Smith	May Robertson
Dorothy Woods	Loretta Nelson	Mabel Stone
Bessie Thomas	Ruth Harrington	Myrtle Feaster
Pauline O' Conner	Edith Howard	Emelie St. Amand
	Josephine Walle	

RICE CAFE AND CABARET, 1501 Iberville Street
(White)

Annie Smith	Mary Spear	Clementime Leford
Ellen Lane	Annie Fernandez	Maggie Russell
	Felicie Fernandez	

VILLA CABARET, 221 N. Franklin Street
(White)

Lilly Muller	Annie Ring	Clara Smith
Eva Boudreaux	Bessie Winn	Bertha Mash
Edna Reid	Lena Swab	Frances Foster

Rose Hubert   Blanche Mathews

The Arlington

THE ARLINGTON

NOWHERE IN this country will you find a more complete and thorough sporting house than the ARLINGTON

Absolutely and unquestionably the most decorative and costly fitted out sporting palace ever placed before the American public.

The wonderful originality of everything that goes to fit out a mansion makes it the most attractive ever seen in this or the old country.

The Arlington, after suffering a loss of many thousand dollars through a fire, was refurnished and remodeled at an enormous expense, and the mansion is now a palace fit for a king.

Within the great walls of this mansion will be found the work of great artists from Europe and America. Many articles from various expositions will also be seen, and curios galore.

PHONE MAIN 1888

225 N. Basin

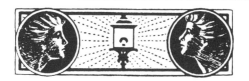

102 RANCH CABARET, 206–208 N. Franklin Street
(White)

Annie Godfrey	Marie Lavigne	Lizzie Zimmer
Rosie Morgan	Gertrude	Camille Gates
Daisy Wagner	Lenoire	Henrietta Penton
Sophie Smith	Hattie Allen	Josephine George
	Gertie Garden	

LALA CABARET, 135 N. Franklin Street
(Colored)

Safronice Carter	Jessie Burney	Jane Pinarba
Mandy Taylor	Alma Hughes	Viola Dalfrey

NEW MANHATTAN CABARET, 1500 Iberville St.
(Colored)

Carrie Robertson	Rosie Gibson	Grace Aunt
Carrie White	Anna Mitchell	Lena Leggett
Ella Williams	Rosie Cooper	Hattie Duffau
	Josephine Robertson	

Miss W. O. Barrera

THIS is one of the few places where a person can visit and leave with the sole satisfaction of having been in the midst of an array of beautiful women who know how to cleverly entertain the most fastidious gentleman.

It has been her mark in life to make friends and keep them.

She also has a most worthy name of being the mistress over one of the foremost sporting places in the Tenderloin District.

Miss Barrera has recently added some very handsome and charming young ladies to her register.

So don't be misled until you have seen this place and the ladies living there.

341 N. Basin

Miss Jessie Brown

This is one of the few places where a person can visit and leave with the sole satisfaction of having been in the midst of an array of beautiful women who know how to entertain properly and cleverly the most fastidious gentleman.

It has been Miss Brown's mark in life to make friends and keep them.

She also has a most worthy name of being the mistress over one of the foremost sporting places in the District.

"Jessie" has recently added some very handsome and charming young ladies to her register.

So don't be misled until you have seen "Jessie Brown" and her ladies.

PHONE 788 MAIN

223 N. Basin

The Cairo

Flora Randella, who is better known as "Snooks," the Italian beauty, is one woman among the fair sex who is regarded as an all-round jolly good fellow.

Nothing is too good for "Snooks," and she regards the word "Fun" as it should be, and not as a money-making word. She is a good fellow to all who come in contact with her.

"Snooks" has the distinction of keeping one of the liveliest and most elaborately furnished establishments in the city, where an array of beautiful women and good times reign supreme.

A visit will teach more than pen can describe.

"Snooks" also has an array of beautiful girls, who are everlastingly on the alert for a good time, and her Oriental dancers are among our cleverest entertainers.

PHONE MAIN 4647

320 N. Franklin

Miss Martha Clark

Is one of the few types of pure Roman Beauties hailing from the sunny shores of Italy.

Martha's popularity has been proven by her success in keeping her house filled at all times.

Her women are well known for their cleverness and beauty. Also, in being able to entertain the most fastidious of mankind.

227 N. Basin

That Dainty Waist

You look so charming in, can be sent to this laundry without the slightest fear of injury. We make a specialty of laundering women's waists and dainty garments so they look even better than when new. Send us a few for trial. After that we know you will have us do your laundry work right along.

American Laundry

Phone Main 346

Branch Agent, BEN VERGES

123 N. Liberty St.

The Club

Pretty Miss Maud Hartman, who has the high position as President of the Club, is one of those jolly fellows who has the support of all those who have joined the Club.

The Club is always open to visitors, so if you have not had the pleasure of a visit, don't stay too long, as you may miss something.

The Club is one of the few gorgeously furnished places in Storyville and is located so that the most particular person can reach it without being seen. It is under the sole direction of Miss Hartman, whom you will find handsome and highly accomplished, and she has nothing but ladies of her class.

The success and reputation enjoyed by Maud in the past is more than surpassed in her new quarters. She has not overlooked anything that goes to make a place famous as well as very select.

Come and join the Club and meet the members.

PHONE 3567 MAIN

327 N. Franklin

Diana and Norma

Why visit the playhouses to see the famous Parisian models portrayed, when one can see the French damsels, Norma and Diana? Their names have become known on both continents, because everything goes as it will, and those that cannot be satisfied there must surely be of a queer nature.

Don't fail to see these French models in their many poses.

213–215 N. Basin

Miss Gertrude Dix

This palatial home was at one time the residence of Miss Hilma Burt, who was noted for keeping one of the best equipped places of its kind in this section of the States.

Miss Dix, while very young, is of a type that pleases most men of to-day—the witty, pretty and natty—a lady of fashion. Her managerial possibilities are phenomenal to say the least, and her success here has proven itself beyond a doubt.

Miss Dix has been with us but a short while but has won all hearts. Her palace is second to none. It is good for one who loves the beautiful to visit Miss Dix's handsome ladies—one can only realize the palace. There are no words for her grandeur of feminine beauty and artistic settings after an hour or so in the palace of Miss Dix.

Miss Dix has an orchestra in her ballroom that should be heard—all talented singers and dancers.

PHONE MAIN 299

205 N. Basin

Miss Louise Dreyfus

Judging from Louise's coterie of friends, she is certainly a lovely woman and one greatly admired.

Miss Dreyfus has proven herself not only a good fellow, but a young woman perfectly capable of conducting one of the very best establishments to be found. Her elegantly furnished cottage is one of the very best in the country.

She also has some of the most beautiful and select girls in the District—one of whom is "Chiquita," the Spanish Beauty.

PHONE MAIN 1417

1310 Conti

Since the days of "GAMBRINUS," a mythical Flemish King of the 13th century, who then was reputed to have invented the first beer: the Brew Masters have worked on the many methods to improve the work of Thirteen Hundred years ago and to-day, you have the

NATIONAL BREWING CO.
OF NEW ORLEANS

BREWING A
Beer de Luxe
In Bottle and Keg

Dos Ist Allies!

Miss May Evans

Miss Evans is one woman among the fair sex who is regarded as an all round jolly good fellow, and one who is always laughing and making all those around her do likewise.

While nothing is too good for May, she is admired and befriended by all who come in contact with her.

May recently erected a handsome mansion in North Franklin Street, that would be beautiful on Fifth Avenue, New York, or on one of the boulevards about Chicago or Philadelphia. See for yourself.

May has the honor of keeping one of the quietest establishments in the city, where beautiful women, good wine and sweet music reign supreme.

What more can a person expect? Just think of it! "Pretty women, wine and song."

In the palace of a king one could not expect more.

The signal of May's mansion is: "Let's all live and enjoy life while we can."

PHONE 1190 MAIN

315 N. Franklin

Miss Edna Hamilton

H AS, without doubt, one of the finest equipped "CHATEAUS" in the Tenderloin District,

As for women, she has an unexcelled array, who, aside from their beauty, are all of high class and culture.

Miss Hamilton is a new arrival, coming from Minneapolis.

PHONE MAIN 4136

1304 Conti

Miss Harriet Holland

While but a late resident of the District, she has gained more friends than the oldest in the business.

Harriet is known as the "idol" of society and club boys, and needs but little introduction, as she is known by the elite from New York to California for her wit and lovliness.

Harriet is very winsome, and appeals to everyone, as she is clever and beautiful. Her mansion is handsomely furnished, everything being the best that money could procure.

Aside from the grandeur of her establishment, she has a score of beautiful women, who, with their charming landlady, form a group that can never be forgotten.

While visiting don't overlook the Holland House.

PHONE 1553 MAIN

1318 Bienville
Cor. Liberty

Mme. Emma Johnson

Better known as the "Parisian Queen of America," needs little introduction in this country.

Emma's "Home of All Nations," as it is commonly called, is one place of amusement you can't very well afford to miss while in the District.

Everything goes here. Pleasure is the watchword.

Business has been on such an increase at the above place of late that Mme. Johnson has to occupy an "Annex." Emma never has less than twenty pretty women of all nations, who are clever entertainers.

Remember the name, Johnson's.

Aqui si hable Espanola.

Ici on parle francais.

PHONE CONNECTION

331-333 N. Basin

TADEMA CIGAR

THAT MADE
JAKE STERN
FAMOUS

CANAL *and* ROYAL STREETS
NEW ORLEANS, LA.

Miss Grace Lloyd

Of all the landladies of the Tenderloin, there are few better known or admired than Grace Lloyd. Grace, as she is commonly called by all who know her, is a woman of very rare attainments and comes of that good old English stock from across the waters.

Grace is regarded as an all-round jolly good fellow, saying nothing about her beauty. She regards life as life and not as a money-making space of time,

Grace also has the distinction of keeping one of the quietest and most elaborately furnished establishments in the city, where an array of beautiful women and good times reign supreme.

Miss Lloyd recently went to enormous expense renovating her establishment, which had been almost totally destroyed by fire.

A visit will teach more than pen can describe.

PHONE 2665 MAIN

338 N. Franklin
Corner Conti

Miss Olga Lodi

Olga hails from Florence, Italy, "The Land of the Flowers," and if all the flowers that grow there are as pretty as the Olga Lodi, then the place must be one of natural beauty or a dream—as Olga is really such.

Nowhere will you find a more complete and better conducted "Palace of Sport" than her "Mansion." Olga has let nothing pass her that goes to make life worth living; so while out, you want to give her place a call if it be only to form her acquaintance, which, I'll assure you, will please you in your meanest moods.

Aside from the magnificence of her home, she has a score of most handsome ladies, who are a "jolly" crowd to be among.

Remember the name:

OLGA, THE ITALIAN QUEEN

321 N. Basin

EMMA JOHNSON'S
''THE STUDIO''

Miss Frances Morris

THIS place is one of the few gorgeously furnished places in the Storyville District, located so that the most particular person in the world can reach it without being seen by anyone.

This mansion is under the sole direction of Frances Morris, who is one of the handsomest landladies in the District and is a princess. Her ladies are of like type.

The success and reputation enjoyed by this establishment in the past is more than surpassed under the able management of Miss Morris, who has not overlooked anything that goes to make a place famous and select.

You make no mistake in visiting 1320. Everybody must be of some importance, otherwise he cannot gain admittance.

PHONE MAIN 2318

1320 Conti

Countess Willie Piazza

Is one place in the Tenderloin District you can't very well afford to miss. The Countess Piazza has made it a study to try and make everyone jovial who visits her house. If you have the "blues," the Countess and her girls can cure them. She has, without doubt, the most handsome and intelligent octoroons in the United States. You should see them; they are all entertainers.

If there is anything new in the singing and dancing line that you would like to see while in Storyville, Piazzi's is the place to visit, especially when one is out hopping with friends—the women in particular.

The Countess wishes it to be known that while her mansion is peerless in every respect, she only serves the "amber fluid."

"Just ask for Willie Piazzi."

PHONE 4832 MAIN

317 N. Basin

"Gypsy" Shaffer

You may travel from one end of this continent to the other, but to find another good fellow as game as "Gip" will almost be an impossibility. To make such an assertion one must be in a position to know from where he speaks. "Gip" is always ready to receive and entertain, and never has it been said that she has not been capable to meet all half way—and leave them all friends.

In going the rounds, don't forget to meet Gipsy, and especially her array of feminine beauties. They are all clever. The head of the house, "Gipsy," will let nothing pass toward making life a pleasure.

Just ask anyone where Gip Shaffer lives.

PHONE CONNECTION

1535 Iberville
Cor. Villere

Miss May V. Spencer

MISS SPENCER has the distinction of conducting about one of the best establishments in the Tenderloin District, where swell men can be socially entertained by an array of swell ladies. As for beauty, her home has been pronounced extremely gorgeous by people who are in a position to know costly finery, cut glass and oil paintings, foreign draperies, etc.

Miss Spencer, while very young, is very charming, and, above all things a favourite with the boys—what one might say, those of the clubs.

May, as the club boys commonly call her, has never less than fifteen beautiful ladies—from all parts of this great and glorious country.

May is contemplating having an annex added to her present home, as her popularity has gained so in the past that she cannot accommodate her friends. You should see her girls.

PHONE 2927 MAIN

315 N. Basin

Miss Bertha Weinthal

WHILE still young in years, has, nevertheless, proven herself a grand woman, and has also made "good" as a conductor of a first-class establishment.

The word of "able" is portrayed in full when the name Weinthal is mentioned.

If it were within my power to name Kings and Queens, I would certainly go out of my way to bestow the title of "Queen of Smile" on Miss Weinthal.

Miss Weinthal is one of the few women who can say she has friends who are friends indeed, and who are with her in all her adventures.

Her "Chateau" is grandly equipped, and lacks nothing to make it the finest in the world. She has lately installed a handsome ballroom.

Pretty women, good times and sociability has been adopted as the countersign of Miss Weinthal's new and costly home.

PHONE MAIN 1326

311 N. Basin

Yes; this is the Famous
Mademoiselle Rita Walker

The Oriental Danseuse, who some years ago set the society folks of Chicago wild about her "Salome" dance. She was one of the first women in America to dance in her bare feet.

Aside from her marvelous dancing, Mademoiselle has a $5000 wardrobe which she uses for her dances.

Mademoiselle is at preseet a guest of MISS BERTHA WEINTHAL, 311 N. Basin St., where she can be seen in her marvelons dances.

Miss Minnie White

MISS WHITE is one of the finest landladies in the District, known to all as a prince of good fellows, always ready to receive you with a smile and pleasant greeting, and counts her friends by scores. She has surrounded herself with a bevy of charming girls, each one a star, who are always willing to meet you half way and make you feel that you are welcome. Once you meet them, return you surely will. Good-fellowship is the secret of Miss Minnie's success.

Miss White has recently added to her array of beautiful women some lively women, entire strangers from the far Northwest, and queens among queens they are.

PHONE 1663 MAIN

221 N. Basin

Miss Alice Williams

ALICE, as all the boys call her, needs but little to tell that she is the mistress of a first-class establishment.

Here is one whole-souled member of the fair sex who is sterling and a jolly good fellow.

No one knows what a good, jovial person Alice is until they have had the pleasure of meeting and forming her acquaintance.

She also has a lot of jolly good girls as guests, who are the "goods" as one would term them. Don't overlook Alice.

1545 Iberville

The Little Annex

Lizette Smith, the jolly and popular mistress of the "Little Annex," is certainly a lovely woman, and one to be admired—which she certainly must be, judging from her coterie of friends.

Lizette has proven herself not only a "good fellow," but a young woman capable of conducting one of the very best establishments to be found anywhere in this country.

Recently Lizette went to great expense in erecting a new home and along with it its furnishings are the costliest French "fine" palaces in America.

She also has some of the most beautiful and select girls in the district, who know how to do things as you like 'em.

217 N. Basin

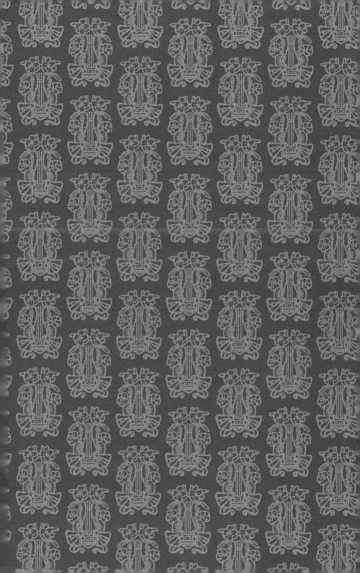